Live Feed

Publication of this book was supported by a grant from The Greenwall Fund
of The Academy of American Poets.

Live Feed

poems

Tom Thompson

Alice James Books

FARMINGTON, MAINE

The author is grateful to the editors of the journals in which the following poems first appeared:

American Letters & Commentary: "Calling Home the Cows"
Boomerang: "Anon. Noir," "Burnt House" (as "Make Yourself at Home"),
    "Conversant" (as "*from* Conversations with Death"), and "Documentia"
Boston Review: "Design" (as "A Small Design, Frost")
Colorado Review: "And a Flock of Pigeons Shall Lead Them"
Fence: "In Loco Parentis"
Indiana Review: "Gullet"
Volt: "Current"

The author wishes to acknowledge his dear friends, remarkable poets all, who offered sustaining support and invaluable criticism during the course of writing these poems and shaping the book—Timothy Donnelly, Lynn Melnick, D.A. Powell, Sam Truitt, Sam Witt, and most of all, Miranda Field.

Alice James Books gratefully acknowledges support from the University of Maine at Farmington and the National Endowment for the Arts.

Alice James Books are published by the Alice James Poetry Cooperative, Inc., an affiliate of the University of Maine at Farmington.

ALICE JAMES BOOKS
238 MAIN STREET
FARMINGTON, ME 04938

www.umf.maine.edu/~ajb

Library of Congress Cataloging-in-Publication Data
Thompson, Tom, 1967–
    Live feed : poems / by Tom Thompson.
        p. cm.
    ISBN 1-882295-31-5 (pbk. : alk. paper)
    I. Title.

PS3620.H69 L58   2001
811'.6—dc21   2001029411

for Miranda

for Willie

for Finnian

Contents

1

Calling Home the Cows

Where night comes in,   the door's growl and fetch.
Crouch to a lower peek,   street light delivered
through the letter slot.   Here, featured, some
darling shoes for you—   backed and streaked
with day's gunmetal   cud. A man come about
a little animal he wants   put together.
Each job's hook is tenderer,   like this light,
like that public sunken shoulder   set to level the door,
your opening blackening eye.   And so you said,
"Come on in, I've been   having a little episode."
You've been having that dream   so ankle deep in blood.
Oh kid among wax paper.   Oh fatty glistening lips.
You need the scratch but no   you're done.
You've already passed on   this offer once—wanting
to slip on a future   like see-through gloves. Just so
the seams crack,   shackles reach down
to the street, liquid, red.   This past mouths abstinence
at you now o proud flesh.   Hmm. Phlegmatic
trucks sit and sputter   outside: the prospect
of solid employ   a vanishment. Consider your own
cooled heels at the zero hour   and how the gibbous moon
stands in for Lips of Fate.   You believed in lasting
work once but the moon's   not talking and you are
just the one cry in the airshaft.   The Booke of Fame
is a many shout.   What made a local boy big
on the small screen: less the familiar way
his glance o'er-threw,   more the way
he punched some lady's thighs   with his silver tact.
Afterwards a sound   like puppets doing "breeze."
Cars at their cow shtick   pacing the downtown
palaver. Big cobble stones   tightly packed,

a script writer's dream!   Et, voilà. Here
where the cattle end   eating cattle, where the feral cat
licks its pillow through   continuous night,
the local boy's pissed,   chucks sawdust over slop
all over the set.   The klieg lights adore him.
Hmm of your own blue monitor,   as the director
off screen and last year   cues the glamour puss
to croon you   and you alone.

The Reverent Cha Cha

We'll bring down the house with a one two, one two three—
herding hassle for a living
and at midnight tonight . . . Whhhat the silken ticking means,

oh city, take this cup from our hand. The door fee's
a piece of smoke. The scuff marks
permanent on the one wallet between us. Such parquet

the past we glide on. Don't drop a drop now, that's me
you're shaking like a fist.
One gesture mistaken for cowardice on the floor and boom

you're it. The lone heel's gunshot echoes. The story
we told ourself gone off
in the entre-act: starring as the invisible lit cigarette, tweezers,

decoder ring, trading cards in pocket. So now we bring them
to their knees. Each step
has its uses, the dead man said; so we did believe.

In this city, wind's beatific hucksterism lures us to fractured
measure, blistery meaning, utter
admittance. Oh, we're good at numbers, at loss

for words. When throwing ourselves over the ground
we plunge the neckline
like a cliff diver with one real move on entry.

Gullet

Awash at the rim of the tidal dark steps
rise up from earth and new earth
descends. Here it is that cloud-hid fiend

shakes your carriage once, again,
threatens at each pause to slip into ether
if you don't.
Walk him by hand, then.
You don't want alone, so you talk, talk, stop, rock, sing

that tonight, maybe he would just Jesus
make of it sleep.
Up ahead there's talk of shadows
meeting, getting lost. Time to hurry on
there to the place you show, what,

light, passage, us? Use anything
to seduce a drowse, caress it in
through that fiend's blank skin,
yours. These acacias you've dreamt of,
leafless redbuds and the slow-begun

push to any close. Who's being dark
about whose business? We take root,
sway. And would take ourselves
liquid in, steep to swallow
and swallow if we had but sleep.

Organicity

Motioning, the storm bank   drops to its knee
in a wall   of glass buildings. Yes,
we unbuckle, unwilling,   assuming
cloud shapes   on the commute.
Cross streets,   underground
junctions, all astream   of the press
of people: whither   are we moved
to move.   Measureless
distance from home   to the work since
this ongoing   is where we remain.
Yes. Above,   one dark cloud tosses
back its hair and we   go blind to see.
Oh, infant sky   with skin peeled
back. Oh, animal   voyeur.
It's sky's lead veins   that smile
these sudden snug hooks: a going
down, a coming   up. We're cracked
pellucid beakers abrim   with salt.
We make passes   in the dirt, dressed
in the gauze of rain's   long white eyes.
Who bears us,   so tenor to city and
hungry, this humid,   such busy corpse?

Item

Another plush factory, boned. Some kid's aching schematic,
    or is this just how structures tend? Our wary

sashay approaches the next green steel pipe, this one arching
    luminous nipples overhead. Tonight's show features

warning lights, all tangle and billow, abdicating, promoting,
    abdicating . . . We're parched, naturally, but non-committal.

Our lips an ingenuous impasto. And now that mean scent lashes us
    still under this flight path of lofty, antediluvian planes.

But newscopters? Gone all tickety in the whisper chapel.
    The highway, just. (What car's that. What car's that.)

Let's you and me travel down the road a click. There
    where a white scrap of clothing flags the clouds

down from their shelf, another life-long feeling
    plops underground. Nor can this maintenance road

contain us. We'll service our own flush, dissolving
    port thank you. Even the vertical girders are dotted

with probability here, evaporating duration itself. And you,
    crinkling. My right eye itch a. A tremor. A fainting

you're too nervous to acknowledge. So, you Weak-at-the-knees,
    you Me, you give? The bag stretched

makes a plastic trigger. Take that wind
　　　down. Husk your blush a notch. There we are,

taut in the line of sight, frank, pluckable.
　　　Who are you. But I. Sirens rise and cross the sky.

Documentia

Skin puckers in this heat, sexing and ugly.
Cut to a tight close-up: sweat forms
pretty white strings of crystallized devotion.
Slow pull back and cross fade
to mourners on site. The star's plane
ever dead spirals in sight of sheer cliffs,
the surf on our screens whipped sugary
beneath a haze of droning sun. Let us become
beautiful images entering dream. Cut to anywhere
life bloodies up without the blood display.
Call it a lost place. Call it tomorrow
and today it is dream's dead mouth and your own
live fingers going down on yourself
as you picture going down on the star
in the suddenly leaden jet and even now
umn ah curtains draw open wide
across the way. Pan to a clear vase
stuffed full of eagerlilies, what marks the spot
where a brittle demon took down the squab
in a clean kill. Does this distract
or call attention to you? Those flowers
were a false stab at discretion, but you love the gesture
like it's a soundtrack. As in grace before dinner,
how it hindfucks hunger. And you are hungry
distractedly, eating this moment
as if it could be eaten through.

Commercial Shoot

May Day rose as a pale imitation. A spent
intervention. We are hardy enough.
With poles our blank
smiling gaffers bicker with the failing sun
and the trees raise ruckus
about the wind.
None of us is equal to the parts
we have been assigned. Let us rise.
It is our father and daughter who bound by.

In the air above our crew the switched-off
glances are mirrored back
without even the doormen noticing—
such shiny apartments around this block. I beg you
for cover, lean into
each frame. The way the talent jogs
thick plates of maple bark
off the lawn is a little too

autumnal. They are on leave. On call. In a meeting.

Generate a family mist
for the city to disappear into.
Oh gunpowder and motor oil,
what a fantastic job! Let us increase.

The Giver of Gifts Knows Nothing
of the Delights of the Merchant

We strive to deflect at a blow the blows
come from the hard, glaring, nameless thing.
We keep handing you, what, we can't see.
You hand back what thing you can.
Say it's the sun if you want.
Say it's some change. None of us
with word one for each other,
relax. No matter here, darkling:
Take that glance off your look
and let us in. Those eyes are your coin
and do a mean barter. But see, there's nothing
comes back to you but our leather hands,
the split wallet's only currency
fit for a machine we are not. Here we are
at the pleasure of the commercial
principle: peddle and hold; disperse
and tinker. Some enlightened nagging
about what we'd do to each other
if we were ever without each other. Ahead
full steam and screw the cows coming home,
hmm, my liege, my darling?
Yes, you could imagine, who practice faithfulness
to the day even as that first infidelity
springs us from your trading pouch.

Glut in the Abattoir

Glint in the moneypitch where silence took you up. "Oh
a clean suckling," says you, or is it another split animal

muttering gutterals— gluttering—. You clear? Flies rip
round your metallic bit doing the can can with a mean

flick & switch. And still the chewed bait retreats as in,
"She loves you not." You all but collapse on a bed of indecision,

a bed as good as any among all this clean lumber, soft cork.
The conveyance device whistles a merry tune. Go on,

bury this last hour of yours. Your patience is already tangled
among the clientbracken. You'll get to talk dirty in a clear spot

later. For now, just maximize your tonnage of pancreas,
flesh it out into quality fertilizer. You're an earthy multiplicand

for a place this steely, a value composed
of disbuted accounts. Splinter or chip, we all go gaseous in time,

it suits the sea change. Just so, your ink-stained meat lick
ascends among fatty air and eveningspangles, the ether

where battlefields dissipate. As there, where the higher-ups
saw at a muscular spread, feast enraptured by the solid breach.

Let your look tower down to the evisceration room where body
blends into sheer matter, matter into blunt performance.

& love lets drop an arborescence. Pause, trickle. Enters your engine
of collapsible virtue, as in one more retreat, nnh, beckon.

You Want

You want, what, a hole in a hillside? A spot
to crouch in? Maybe a green space above you
with stone built round. Your body
used to be transparent-like. Now,
all unwilling—white flag of flesh
in the way of commerce. This is a stream, right?
This water with its hair on end. You want
to fall in, sip it right through your lungs,
but tiredness only brings you back to the world.
You want some of that bird's gray-green feathers
to patch through with (wind's doing
its whipalong). But through to what? Arrival?
End of the line? In this city? The green heart
you want is at light-speed on blades,
soot-slick. You put the cat down in the middle
of the park to look for where there is
left to go. He crouches low. Nowhere left
that isn't low, under sun, that is . . .
iridescence flickers by . . . Spot reflections,
maybe, or prehistoric pigeon flutter
in historic crags, or oil making a window
of sky's watery surface tension.
In your eye's corner there's what animal
is still inside your bones. Who, chewed into, chews.

The Sun Is the Country Wherever He Is

The air's too solid, drips down your cool front.
But you sing like you want, with mouth shut
to the people here, these foreign bodies
squatted about with packet luncheons.
Their dear bags of heatedly bought knick-knacks
swell to a lapping tide, ring out from you.
Who blew that whistle? Who called us to gather
and now's gone?—scarring us like
a weather front that faltered. Whispered
gauze where you got slicked by the gone wind.
Haze melts you and you into haze. You got culled
then frayed then loosed by this glaring thing
you have no time for. Oh, you want,
I know you want. But what of that? What
locked heart's been picked by your eye's keyholing.
The linen swish you followed? How about what
it so revealingly failed to lead to. How about those
precious metals that send light back across the park
in neck-level glances. Is their still-kissed gleam
getting at your wherewithal, you working
for that light now? Your eyes answer blankly.
At the sun's direction, you wear your own face,
only, of course, starring now as the sun.

Jerusalem

Is this the city then? It's gone all bright and narrow,
twisted, commonplace. Of course,
your eye's got to broker its own light—
you stick to the shade now. Palm and palm
unfolds what looks like welcome in a speech
you'd give anything to learn or tongue
for its water. You keep fanning out odd bills,
but still can't figure it. Shut it,
shut. The sun duns, outworld wavers. Laughter
pools out from a stall you didn't know was there
and may not be tomorrow.
Is that sheen native to the board? Too sheer,
too laid out and languishing. Each object's open
to light bicker and rub. You could buy a blouse
for the lover you picture an ocean away
picture her lifting it to another's touch . . .
This transaction's but echo, right? Tight echo,
thin as your shirt. As that guy boiling bitterleaf tea
against the heat in some local custom,
or maybe a tourist's. Such bright teeth
soothe you, his barbed cheek cracked lips godly
ticking 'king cloaked as an entering tongue.

The River

1.

Alight among the afternoon river, penned & sullen underneath,
      the surface drag stills. Under the visible,
at the visible, the flow folds and tucks in light for later fish.

      Who knows when the thruway racket will quit fussing
with the air? Or when that boy on the wharf will finally thread
      his shark kite through the falling sun? Your love is perched

nearby, tries to plot the arc of your attention even as the wind
      sifts through, hungry for the next tin body.

2.

      To hold and to dispense is river's will. The featureless
fact of clouds mirrors the boy's face, sleeping in the car.
      He's strapped in his own skinpocket of whir and click.

The sleeper's eye scratches at the fulminant when, says *This is the
      skiff's dream:* the tug at surface glass; undertow's see-thru
suck, mottling, down to bed. But whose boats plot the river?

      Whose mast holds the sky firm while sun plays at husk?
The day moon's up, echoes the bent horizon and the unsure notes
      of the boy's mother. This is a low sky to be in to be sure.

3.

The cars continue that the boy reaches for in his new-fangled
      theory of outside: diving bird, flying fish, classifications
for the endless and broken surface. No more definite left,

only wingspan and the shedding of water's frank tension.
Glint on shadow, meat taken whole and disembodied. All just
one more causeway. And on, innumerable windows

offer themselves up in a burning paean to seeing. Take us
for atmosphere, then. One by one down to the bone zero.

4.
The river is a fluid solid, uncoiling like a snake as it swallows
each live thing. Speed is a kind of housing says the sun.
Take it down like light it still is slow. Take it down. The cars

will rush you, the trees will, but still they move too slow.
The river blinks, ditches the shore while out from under
Heaven's scales a corps of bees hem & swim, pure verb

setting forth a particle play at sundown. You want to live,
and live. As you shine on wet rocks standing in
for the rain & sleet to come. Who can tell where wind may lie,

how the wish of the bed is for bed again.

2

The Pool

The canary green glass surface goes roil and smoke
from the trees's retreat from the feet and feet
coating it in a flat rug of buzzing swirls
of beings lifting inches off the water
in light undulations of movement—*ready set
glint*—the magic carpet of sun's return to sun.
Makes one think you're still trying
to close in on the sky, while the rocks
you pocket plunk and bulk. The weedy shadows
fold their hips from needle to embrasure,
mirror your daddy-hand's hook
for a worm-pale finger. Out over the skinny track
that runs along you're dogging a runner
to flush the quiet, the pair of you
chase and lose, more -being than not-.
Each glance shot at a silent spot. The eyes
are too blunt, they snap shut and plug.
Freedom's a fickle rush, slash-bed
and layer. Anymore, you'd both surrender.
Cut open-toed through the shallows, then,
back up along the hill popping with bait.
Beetles cling all the same
while the bark just kisses back. A set
of coppery corpse-wheels could make it
this distance, only the rising fear
that you've come too far
too deep in your enjoyment.

Cup of Drift

A lapsed-down silt drifts in under the clotting
algae nets. Spiders map the leaf-pressure
until a finger so pink and peculiarly mine
pops each spun line with one fingerforearm shot.
No musk point as heft but flesh
simply as it follows muscle. Or you,

distant driver's mind behind a wheel,
pluck digit-like nails to build and buttress a house with.
The riverbank's sun-smashed peat
plans collapse but battens down instead
now plush-folding into tomorrow's trail
as dusk twines

down like clouds. You crossfade
to a wine dark liquefaction
(thunderhead hovers, whistlings still)
while the boy expands to fill any space
breaks it open unh in the viewing compartment
like a kidney bean makes for itself
out of a cup of dirt. Evening's absent rush.
Hudson, bottle, squirrel and stranger
you always fail to reflect us whoever we are,

whoever it is applies us to each river's tine.
The sun snaps one last piece of itself
off again. Wind? Bangs me flat
into a flicker up from the pavement.
Only now can the skin plant
get at its beckon and surrenderings
which attest to each arching back,
yours and mine, buckle and weave.

Richard Kimmler's Cottage

The found thing's skin singed back
to a lapsed panoply of tendon. Swollen,
powder gray, licked entrance and exit
for a florid, grating engine, a carotid
air. Ticklish, mechanical sequences
of bee and been stitch the rising ridge
these blank pages in your opening
coaxed by a few hairs.

Our build, too, brightens.
A conscious incantation of color and form
explodes above the body
as a pear tree, buzzing against
the northern hills. The impossibly white
blossoms rattle into strict tongues

that you will not succeed. Stop surrendering
what comes to us. Split bark
and spilt paving stone, a whipped-up wind
through loose grass: one part

threading another, now loose, now tight,
drags us to a standstill. The carcass
pulls sky close as westerly the ground
sinks and the shelf of you reachcracks,
vanishes like sand into faulty hearing.
Do we shrink from nearness? Rise from it

all glassine sugars, slender and cutting. Your speed
is equal to the angle of that bone.
There you go. Lids shut. Mind miles back

and shut—trying to stake in the nausea of an opening
life even as it wills itself into your bloodstream.
Clouds picket the impassible ceiling. Might the next

range have something for us? It's an ocean away.
Sunlight and porch-shadow punch and twirl
into a dance that's all wrong—
negation reeling with position as one

creature to the kitchen door now asks with four hands,

Won't you feed here too?

By Reason of Appetite

The neck-nerve begs for it—as in roses, forsythia,
prickly flowers of our most fanatic persuasions.
Oh, molly-coddled heart and greenriverspleen,
your sunny back watteaus up
on the cooling rack like morning tarts,
or was that last week?

Forehead to forehead, we give and take
into the fleshpress of insatiable folly.
Let us begin at the clavicle—only,
weak and weakening I radiate from the liver out.

There is reason in the appetite of flies,
kef of other-flesh. This is not arbitrary
as soon as it is placed at the end of my finger.
The good son peels me back
like a godhead with a job to do, cell by cell,
only the pulse left to reveal itself.
Shrouded in myth or just a shroud—remaining
engine of the Let Us Begin. Chugging.
Chirping. Chipping in.

Our Lady of Perpetual Drizzle begs for a downpour
as we up then down then doze through
once more. How bright the world might be
if only we could reject it outright.
But this morning my stomach contracts
about its acid-clear lightning. Inkblot
assumes the eye, the trickle of last loves
all about our nuclear bud. Now,
there's thunder for you (but you can't
hear it you can't hear it you can't hear it).

Quarry

No motion among the nude crew of us, strewn
so beautifully about the granite quarry—
just subcutaneous chit chat from dirt
gumming loose rock, from our sinew and tissue
as they ping and hold for us these fastidious
dick-down, ass-high poses. It's all
so piecemeal this job, modelling for future
campers, figuring lichen's flair, granite's
pinkening. Oh, pretty edible, says our counselor,
discretely. Trees these hills ripped off
from da Vinci picket the estate. Roughly:
We are all too pure idea and too present,
whatever the busted map says, or said.
But this was never your intention. "Sin
is not a negation, but a position." Someone
laughs. I don't want to know about it. Clinka.
Clink. Sloe gin or sunbars, sharp and shut.
Wouldn't have seen you but for that passing
flight—shadow progress on the still machine
where the eyeflick caught you,
though it was meant for something else.
Some zero device this "ever after." Even
on that top ledge, it's a false lift and over
a shadowy prize. Underneath,
there's faint scarp along the professionally
decayed back-scenery. This is where
the rotund, creeping organ should start,
doesn't. But a good chunk of skyline flashes
signals to us about some touchy meandering,
another flighty, slow start to quickening under
hide and sand. Jesus I'm tense. Well, aren't we
just pure idea now. Hold it. Hold it.

Lit

I know the hot line running through my deathpoint,
friend of my enemy and my friend.
Liquid as fire. As these shifting fields
where I track the lit effigies. Glinting,
crushed glass refracts each handheld direction.
Rivery footlights careen across organ mass,
crawl through shadow grass
over keep-out wire and keep-in wood,
up to the oak's shimmery autumnal negligee.
The branches' blood is a sticky neverrun sea.
Cold. Humid air molded, fashioned
and fast as if latched by eyehooks
across our womanly gown's back. Skin's buckled us
about the skeleton: a nice tight waist
where cameras look. Keep it simple,
the eyehook says, holding one more round target
for the spur, begging speed—not quarter nor devotion—
for the kick among shouts, the torn torched clothing.
Our parents are ascendant in the far mob,
meat-based, spinning their ax at the watery pour.
Let me be smoke funneling fleshwise
and I might love these white booms and black ferns
that bed us flat against the downs
with fire and shadow for a mat.

Pluck and Anti-Pluck

What do you hope to gather here? Fear rings you like a bell, too big. Take your strategic clouds back, even the fade to web distillate. All about us the word "children."

( )

A silk skirt hitches, folds up, hatching shadows in the presence of our captive bee. The bee fidgets its toes in envy of the junkethawk's harked-outside looks, hooked claws. Our messenger:

( )

He refuses to rise, one-eyed and fearful. There's an escape map at the talon, rolled and licked like Auntie's cigarette. Rumors of moisture flood the inky routes.

( )

Out, shallow and fast, like years, like someone else again. Nothing but to release what you know to the lagoon oaks and spider moss: a speechless suction.

( )

Awhuzzing where the pavement circles back: molten pebbles go asunder under us. Leaving so many stars on the marsh-top. So many ticcing, lickety stars.

( )

The trees acting as loose shunts between earth and sky, they ran-
kle us. If we're to believe, we need more.

( )

Take speed over silence: one agrees (a falcon) to miss the mouth
breathing at 200 paces. The measure of.

( )

Distance condenses in the far voices of crows, cast like barbed
wire about our bodies. Nice sharp handles, but oiled for burial,
dear.

Conversant

Hold forth you no-eyed leer. Your love is off
with the mortal child you wriggled at,
imagined as a Yes. And her heart leaps
from the ledge of you to the boy to you.
If only at last you could say, REST.
Take an arm, take a leg while you're at it.
That's some woman you're pulling,
the kid pulling—each halving the other's portion
until love disappears, open-mouthed into air.

(   )

You've longed like Achilles for a corner office,
and there's one now in the ether.
She's left you to breathe. The rest of day
is morning at its scaldingest. Ah, steam.
Ah, gloved air and gale of declension.
Your pink papery years browned on both sides
by her lit skin. So, you love. You love!
Now the darkling rend where sky was.

(   )

And all along you pour yourself in little cups,
a crafty dispersal. So keen to battle back the sun
you'd swim with the spleen, but it's not talking.
If only you could fit, efficient
as an hysteric, everything you dread into a body.

Pitch

Its plea is simple, less so when it calls you
father too. You could turn and grumble,
too old too old. But always the insistent,
irreversible claim. There is only the room
swaddled in meaty breeze, a sea's
saturated breath. Go ahead,
stand at the mouth of evening
with an open hand. Let's walk aways
together. Come. Come on. It shakes its pelt,
cocks its maw. You two pas de deux,
knuckle and snort back and forth along
these quiet walls (the shriveled body there
still for once). No master
loves more than you. Now, just put
the fiend down, put it down—despite itself,
your wife, your arm and leg. Nothing
will start until the roof hews
cracks among us. The plummet line's still taut.

Flicked

It's been a cool, bad night. The bodyframe
shrieking and flipping itself.
Its many legs, the needs that scale
our skins the length of this
greased bed. I belong neither here nor there.
Allied with the flash
that flickers in and out of consciousness
now, teeth bared, keeps me
at a wild distance. Its lip
reaches at us for primped aureoles, draws us
dry, forward, gnaw unto gummy gnaw.
The body is here to settle us, make milk
of us, as the hole in my bucket
widens, widening . . .
I am not complete, not yet separate. Neither
end nor beginning, I become the
descent, the razor-sharp vanishing.
Whole days, years scraped out of me.
And in my shortness of breath I turn
to this one, mouth to its mouth,
and it's not teeth I feel nor tongue,
it is my own breath parceled out to me
with sticky, particular fingers. And, yes,
it's the only way now. The only ever.

Work Song

Long since alas, my deadly swannish music

Here, what you want.
From the buildings is loneliness.
Happily they provide.
Furry red tops slicked under gray bonnets.
The sparrows are hungry.
In a nit-picky kind of way.
Their dreams of a republic scattered.
Like so much seed, mmm.
Oh well-a-way, a-well-a.
This is not their song.
The grass is new, new and cut.
Given the air whole hog.
A man loose in his torn skin.
Tries to make angels in the glass shards.
Leaves sprouted from the ground.
My darling, my legions.
You rest under the dew.
Over the cock's crow wherever there still is one.

Anon. Noir

Less heart, it disappears down the brick path.
I'm cool. I'm part of what seeming de-
generates into. Oh, my darling
how do we maintain? With the wind
whipping, my heart begs for a bed as in
Lay down pithy lucre, lay down your sweet head.
Oh, pocketful of sea salt, for prayer
blanket, rye.
Give me a light, suddenly becoming
a flick of the mettle as in *What*
sunless vigil. Set the clock to sleep,
then what? Collapse on the table
with a fold of the cards? Worry our bothies
for proof in the purchase?
If the hour is not to your liking,
I will take the infant down
past the park to the sea—where wakes dissolve
into moon's lead cage. That's our face,
love, buried in night's thighs. The air ex-
changes itself for a goodly solid.

Easter Tide

It's a dead day so I don't go out.
All week I pictured my hand on another breast
and yours appears. A signal. A way of
putting things straight. The sky is uniform,
believe me. A sway jacket, this buttoned-up
corpse. The children say, it's a dragon
and eats all the people. The children say,
now swallowed people are dragons too. I am
unadorned, hitched to you at the traffic. That
unyielding flute wires our ears to the airshaft
with its lead pitch. Tell me again the way
my smell rehearses me. How the sky
cellophanes this city with busy design.

Burnt House

You and love shuck pasts like cicadas in halls
you haven't roamed for years.
Shouldering one another's weatherfronts
room to room, crackling like a pickaxe. So what
if your looms and lunges recall a father's bad balance,
his unsure conscience? So this becomes
just another dream's poor geometric proof, confirms
your age and the lastingness of house. There's still
a slapped-up wall out by the garden,
the rope eeked through a knot in the pine.

Grip and scramble up to survey the same split trunks
and shrubs you once used for hideout. Why this return
to abandoned memory sites? The rejected ways
include the parlor, the once upon a brunette boy,
that unknown cousin cued up on green felt.
You're still youngest and a catapult
cranked full back with fear. Aiming at what,
indifference? The loss you want to become?

Bright plastic pieces dislodge from memory
like stray saw teeth, cross-cuts
to the jaw. Who can stop them?
If only your once and present fury
could devour mind's formlessness, ash descend
into patterns we could climb out from faster.

A Wake

You're rigid at last, starched not against gusts per se
but still apt to collar them. There's a white sheet
of wind that works through, glances off
the low stone village—
what makes for a partial reference
as it whips tent flaps and curtains, rails
against grass stubs, slams shut
our human voice. That's your vault lid's gold
capped with a sheared-out horse logo,
clumsy, fragile, tin. You turn
to the meat shard your hand's become,
I think it's you, and with a free arm secure
your offering with the others . . .
which the crowd takes for gesture, as in grace.
Or maybe you're just singular,
beat-back-the-crowd vanitas. What are any of us
doing here among the land-locked? Your forehead
slips down nicely thank you, steely
and calibrated. The sun doesn't want to hear about it,
but you're liege to a seam—where clouds tip
the blue back, gulp it down.

Design

Frost at midnight needle-points the windows
above us and on every side. Is this what pins me?
The windows do shake, the heat does rise
from roads and the layers of roads under them.
Is that the trap? I wake with words,
I sleep with words, and still I cannot speak.
It's a trick of the jaw. The skull itself conspiring
to keep me just short of you. Here, the question of merge
and the points in our bodies that play at being able.
That lie down for the other, baring the neck
to so fine a set of blade and bone.
What you carry inside, you carry
as if a cradle, a back and forth and not ongoing.
There we are, you'd say. Already
it escapes us—ribs split for the foot,
then the head, stretch of skin, sin and muscle,
that third of us munching seawater like grass.
Is this the way out? So I ask, so I am bound
by stranger flesh. Until the drivetrain slips,
until the sirens arrange themselves
into a pattern one can sing, the stars left to steer by
will be cold. The design, we say,
is greased, slips from us. Who put me
here is you. Who left me here is me again.

The Realm

Where night stops in a tidy pocket of time
is woven from the chromeplush chords of busses
pushing at the traffic. Let us be brief in this—
time for the feed, time for the loop.

Is it the train underneath that fissures?
The train retreats, and we move east
where the water is. East and rising
out of the waveless calm the clammy suits
approach, Our Men of Me, clamber
through the circles spirals jetties
commerce builds up where foot and grunt
stick to the swirling banks dissolve
to the river's currently beautiful woman
who calls herself last ditch.
We sense a non-transferable zero we can't
take our eyes off.

The body's horizon line surrenders
to blistery activity. The self-hunger of seeing
takes on the bent and stun of a bulked up steer.
Let us turn to the silk man in the robe
who faces us each morning
from the boat, in the bath, over the damned stove.
Now for that shiny buckle, the silver
glints our teeth make.

Stir

After the sunspot of daybreak comes dream:
you fussing at a locker poolside,
ignoring a man doing laps. The water ticks
like your skin from the disease he carries.
Mid-stroke he goes, What is it?
And you make to answer, knowing him now
as your friend. Stop, he says, just.
No sign but the ticking
as it takes after desire, no,
the sex, a rift, or, blood, as you into world.
You took your parcel of risk once, too,
what you put away, just put.

All along you're by the little metal door, trying
to figure it. For some it swings,
others, slides back, for you
it won't budge. Where's the combination?
First kiss? First penitent fuck? No. The sequence
was still on your wrist then. Years
fog and envelop a vein that calls out
and away. Fickle narrative, this.

Your first last love all spent, slowly,
that part of night. It's barren fields,
the gone-off gun. You getting pieced apart, no?
Waked by plummed fingers, pricked nails,
it matters what you say next.
Whether your unlidded memory helps lose or find
this friend on that coast.
Morning's clear gray fluid embalms. We call

what follows, looking. Your friend
looks the same way at different water.
In such throat, a flash sprig of dust
could do the trick—nor leaves the passage be.

Bearing

Awakened in a crack, high in stone, blackened
soil for sheet or sheet for soil. It doesn't matter.
Either way I was unhanded, defaced
with richness. Neither minutes nor hours
put me there, just height, and the inability to land.
Below simply unwilling to lend my body flight.
Was it your realm or not that loomed then,
woven out of unseen clouds—unseeing—destroyed?
Too mine too, the icht in night knocked and left.
My feet kingly to a humbled head. So unlike,
I snapped sleep in two, its cane, unstrung
its leash. You bled some as we made our way
out among the thighs, no more wondering. Me uh. Me a.
Storm kissed glass of skin, yours or mine,
the out-wet in. You slipped into rising ice
midsection of me. The mistook pull now love for fright.
There was no weight like sound. No measurement
meaning last tick, first click this clutch
at breath and now begun. Unwilled and willing
in another body's protracted kingdom, ocean of undersun:
Percuss it. Percuss. Midnight frayed. Light
gone grainy into loops of unkempt tissue, violet
at the edges, making for violent figures,
the endless sight behind shut eyes. Always
and again the cells require it.

3

Interregnum

Coughed to life at the jet   gray-blue wraiths growl
and beckon either side of the boat.   Who-made-the-engine
ravening on about some   untoward business. Time we made
a play for the far bridge,   sure. The twilight fish
run the gulls along—   a white wafted shit
kissed at our river's corrugated   seam. Such flash parading
solos, such petty theft   pleasure-speckled
like a gold waistcoat.   And did the shore dogs ask
to throttle at the dirt wire?   And Who-made-us
to breathlessly mouth arc arc?   Divine geometry's
too clean to capture anything   but what's beyond
our palpable sight.   Here is the stock wandered-off.
The infant dressed as   (remember now) translucent
wailing wall, towerly   tempest of hobbled weather.
We cannot hear it   only because it has our voice.
Ground's calypso-jiggle   we don't feel so much as note—
tremolo-tidewater,   soil-trace sky. The signal
for day's end scattering   opaque clouds
the same signal as for begun.   Who-would-outlast
blows open memory's glass measure—   slapdash
circumferences of the lip   we did ring and tongue.
What's not and is still here   battens. Slipknot
of a said thing—   that would give direction a little
head. Hmm, yes,   that's it wind, that's it right there.

In Loco Parentis

My mind for world is   fleshy ground, and so
begins a slight tremolo   no one noticed before
but my darling,   my darling. She always swan
dives into the No   where skin was. Into
the frigid burge   of blossom we think of
as "spring," and as now   even with the sleet
slicing air.   I am tired. I am nomad sagged.
What carries me   through water is Yes
I'm tired. Bump. Bump.   Fresh out of dregs,
I collapse, as my love's   bodily want
skeleton-keys my frame.   "Toughen a likely
thread," I tell myself.   "Surround the stray tooth
with your hands up."   The tooth spreads wings
and is not a tooth.   Blushfully active. Abliss
and bucketful.   It is an anger and crow.
I give it my hands, my feet.   I am not particular.
Knees crumble, lips   wax. "Unusual,"
my love thinks,   "but not unheard of."
Butterflies land on my head,   now the stump
where the foot was.   Non-sequential sequins
glitter me, glitter mine.   They have us
right where I want.   I can't stop
giggling. Imagine!   That it is thou a boy
& I a son, each the   other's pink, pliant
cause. Lift,   squirrel and gnaw. I am
the more the more   in your chewed basket.

And a Flock of Pigeons Shall Lead Them

To the skyflare flurry   the boy hands back
the thing, the thing   in his hands remains
hot. The sun's behind it,   sure. The boy grows
equal to each parent's   misgiving and surpasses
his own joy. Who are you   blue rage and idle
winged? You left midnight   with holes in your shoes.
Left the shoes there pushing   for the stairs. The
ten thousand doors   shut. The goods fenced.
Our boy's hungry   not to eat. His thirst gathers
for the dropperful of ocean   that passersby pass on,
that you hold in your cells.   And that father
who ripped the word   *each* out of us accrues
a flashy debt they call   irrevocable, thing upon
thing singing scorn. You   want this boy to settle
the account he scuttles.   The talks go back long
into night. Echolalia   the only way we continue
to continue. This   arrangement has no hope
of completion   which makes you tomorrow's
patron (called say   father) (of a sudden).
Not a word is   to be breathed. The boy's a leak
of day. His toes show   through. His hands
a diptych of forgiveness   then fistfuls
of nervy static,   our flickering reception.

Aqua Regia

Outdoored, the thick, dogged fingers
of a gone and coming sun tap

where this wharf is nailed shut and nailed shut.
Now sudden pivot, as the platinum-dun

light takes a breather from the boy—
who tackles the darkling promenade,

that kingfisherly boy. He's gentled
and strapped in susurrous citying, so

wild-eyed in great coat and shoes all
ajumble. Who could fail getting

winded over these planks? What's left
unblown? Unbent to the eye

flag staff punches a held-out stub of air.
The city's been up sharpening

its teeth again. Its pleasure wings
the ground: blue, silver, black and green

hitched to the water's throat.
There's a bite-size verdant patch

in the distance. A spot to settle
the eye, say, while the river takes

its knives out to the morning's fat boats.
Wherefrom glances hurry

shoreward. Somewhere back behind
the goldening traffic a cat pursues

ticking, the day moon, all its costly directives.
What takes a breather from the boy

wanders back. As new weather hangs
solvent over our face. Notshadow.

He's hissing again, the sun, hands riding
shotgun. River a kind of counter-

solution: to the eye dissolving up
as a ghost over the liveried city,

a straw witch lit in the dawnthrum.
Surroundings' beckon beat and surge,

oh people, here is the given ground,
the feat we beg release from.

Each Form a Day Takes

Windows? No. Staging. The transparency
offered, revoked. A tricky pause. An etched
trail of swallow-tails disappears
in the particulate light above us and behind. Here
is the sound of plush below Vermeery glass
and Canal sawing its way to the tunnel.
We want back off this island as much
as we both want that painting, no that one, yes
buckets of red ripped and sloshed into.
However fill our belly you can briefly imagine
beginning the begin in hot pants
and leopard prints. Well, as easily
as it could begin in line breaks and periods.
The layaway approaches. Stop. The meaning
ricochets. Stop. The finale rodeo is circling
circling in on its bright tricycle, starring
our own son. And junk sales? Benign! Leaves
fall as the light lifts and branches
sway back. A flat dress is strung among
the patterning squares, billows. A lithe
documentation of ingress and inexactitude.
You hearten a bit early. (Forgive me.)
We're getting hungry with winter coming on.
Your every move frays my leash. Out
and abounding gravel makes the day falter,
more easily trod upon. Like the coming night.
Like the music you bought to dance to before me.
With you? With you. With me. Without.

April Entries

I know very well how the day starts,
shut, swollen with dew. Thus
the dissipating dream, my collarbone squeezed
by a giant anaconda nicknamed "Love."
Well, "squeezed"—bent back, inched back
soundlessly along kitchen tables and desk lamps,
bunk beds and ground cushions.
So many greased things of the world!
And each so perfectly suited to its task.
Me filling up spiral-bound notebooks with writing
that mimics the foot-patterns of pigeons—
marking time. But until what?
Don't answer that. Blushing at the thought
of morning light, I prepare myself
for nothing more. Think how you held that daughter
with those long thin fingers, how they grew
in strength. Tendons cracked, spread.
But she paid no mind, intent
instead on the priest's low robes, and the priest
on passing a silver cup that nips and bats
at the hair. It doesn't take much
you know. One cold rumor in the body these days
and the whole plant shuts down. Light
takes the lid off, sniffs, then seals us up again.

Sacristy

Down among the sweltering wicker you bead
like spittle, swift and heavy as enzymes.
Your fore-cheeks remark only a whiff
of emptiness, like breath, like its lack.
There is no matter here, just the local-stone face
that fronts church offices. Each block
has been driven square, like your knees,
by a decision hit upon again and again. All rise.
It may be you don't recognize the hinge
that's your own breast bone—how it flaps
as thin as a wing, a door—
the field being what it is out here, a circuit board
of invisible breathings. The world out front
may once have shaped you, but now
seems only to fork up & down. Right turn,
left, too, give way too easily;
there needs a little push-against to give bearing.
Please exit this way. There are no
guards to report to, directly. You may once
have been told that a light record gets expunged.
Nice, you may think. You may think, Who?
Keys get frantic about your fingertips;
a mule leers at you in the distance.
What a mucusy place you've wrecked on.
Emollient-based. Imperilled as singsong,
it's called a hook. It's culled gravity.

Cease Thou Never Now

Sumer is ycomen in, / Loude sing cuckou

Before the night hill   topples we come to
& pause. The boy   loses himself, pouring
water into water.   Red oak leaves still
recede from the window.   What choice do we
have in the manner   of happiness? The boy
distributes particles   of sleep like jarring
rumors. Scattered times   chance diminishings
irrespective. We've come   for plaint of birds
cars grinding plane and   sky a single swish
a hem. Who can tell   where answer threads
through the heart or   through the head?
A pressure hard come by   as in, under the drink.
Is this the true seam?   I am tired, a blink,
my skin sings   its layered song. If the
muscles fatigue,   if my wife gathers
my nerves for a little   picnic, how far
can she walk them   before they break leash?
Or will they simply want   themselves out
and into her as they do   each night in sleep's
slit flapping tent?   All is quiet here as
the sea claims sound is.   So walks midnight,
then continue. Looking   for nothing
but steps, finding   none other, my ex-heart
gets hit by the one and the one   until a yes too
would crack it.   And in the burrowing lake
a frog lays bare   his keen, gelatinous
back. The loon begins   his savage bit. Here
lies fatherling with   a word in his pocket, his
imagined promise. Yes   and we break for it

like dirt—   into the ha teeth, the
crocus whir and fall.   Tonight, night. The son,
too, will be shortly at it.   Is this where
we want night to fall?   The undersun gone
all white and lordy.   Fish start we spring
back. The breeze so: handy at us.

A Humor

It starts with a voice calling out from another room.
Out on the ledge eleven flights up,
the other room becomes trees, white and pointillist
below you. So even the trees are taking a position. No:
a piece of darkness falls, quickly rises.
Catch it by your nails, tug it back. It flaps
against your breastbone terribly, until you press
a bit deeper. A first snatch for your purse.
Glances pass window to window into a net—
connecting the nudie shows we compete in
across the avenue. Strangers coupling: you
coupling. Harnesses getting soaped up
in the backroom among the sticky substance
stored in airtight canisters. Cars slip silently
into the storm even as the storm slips
into an ether dream. The leftover pieces
belong to someone else: thigh winched up,
meandering toe, sea-weed hair aligned
with accident, only accident. A toddler seems
to sympathize, but refuses to reveal his thoughts,
repeating yours back to you continually
as his own. The cat remains at an incline
out by the kitchen door, keening
into his metal slab. Shadow descends heavily
onto the ledge, does a dead-on
of having caught something. (You. Not you.)
The caught thing looks free: lolls,
tongue out, hind swaying at a plains pace,

the gray-white face burnished
by a life prowling footlights. Its grease paint
strikes the undercrowd into irrevocable
summons: Ha ha. Ha. Hahahaha.

An Opening

Open the door and roundhouse confusion swings in
until too late you spot the beast half-in-
half-out-the-window to the ledge, swooping
his back down where the slipped window
has stopped unshut,
enacting your recurrent guillotine-dream
even as death creates motion
creates surrender us unto each other

where later there is only out past on the ledge
the gray-broken-into-white feathered layers of wing sparkling up
a granite nest of shit and vomited seeds
green plastic potsherds and mossy bits of sky-ash,
all that entombs the frozen careen
even as the expelled and fluid lassitude
secretly returns to govern with one last phosphorescent eye
out among the bright shrapnel
that dulls us daily as we pick through
color-coded toe tags each one the yellow

of the first down sprouted from that uncertain bird
who'd only later adopt qualities too like metal
and frangible through procedures as playful
as when you and love lie back to back
to classify or talk around another brokening
such as this or that the wind might let down its breasts
let introspection enter exile in the name
of one good eye ear nose throat all those bodily
configurations we doom to you beauty you,

as once we went down we went down
our pleasure maws gaping.

Domestic City

The boy's in the bath,   lacy bubbles lacing
his skull. A soap   crow rises into air,
albino ash.   Rub a-dub. Outside
some guy so piss-drunk   and furious I say *Hail*
Marys for being   too many flights up. There
he is. boom.   at the window. no. boom.
his voice. It will take   longer I imagine
before the people   come over to talk
yew trees and   politics. Oh, the forsythia
is at attention   already. I know a man
who shuts the windows   shuts the doors,
I have to go out   to find it. But today?
Where do you turn—   petty thief, peckish
bird—for lunch? (Cough) (cough)   won't leave off
leaving me. "I am king   of my desire,"
the boy states, a lie   frank as kindling. I am
lonely. A treacherous   breed, tendered so.
The boy the castle we   whistle working at
like wind. In luminous scrawl,   *Today marks*
the millennial month   *of this captivity.*
The idea extends   down the arm, reaches
wick and fizzle   scores the skin. Who
are you, dear? I've seen you   out smoking,
our hands' cupped   *o* the eye's snapped lead.

Demiurge

Yes, I hold you—not by the scruff,
but the way earth holds air.
This is what you take for eternity. What exists
about the bee like a bonnet. And still
the trying to say, I control this, this is mine.
You're ready to lie wakeful and wet
with what you don't know,
clutching either side of the bed, folded up
over yourselves to get away from each other—
there we might last and sleep.
Yes, I love you, but the woods are gone,
the ways I call myself to world
all bunched and twisted, metallic
and stung full of primary colors. Streets thrum
underneath with the power of each
of the 24 hours, hours thick as thieves,
and cars thick as mind. White mind
in pursuit of its end with robe on and make-up,
tired, dear, and tried.

Current

The river strikes sparks off the sky, a stranger's
gold skin knifes back and apple-pleasure

plummets. Evening seeps up from
a curved darkness. My weak skin on point,

then sits. Good boy. Is it hunger
that keeps me? I am my weight, in blue drag.

The liver puts on its slovenly face. It is
my only angel. And in the wind, that is

my Lord, a way to stop, a way to breathe
through the dying fall.

There is the bodily rise and bob. New heads
flickering past like ash—*psst . . . pssht . . .*

The daily glide of the given-up (in memory
as in water). My daring always was

for the concrete. You are another ending
who lick smoke off love's fingers ahmn

mine. Fickle tongue, true
hands, no leash shorter than wakefulness.

Crossing the Horizon

The day stretches its arms too wide and we
regain course. It is not we

who sent us, nor released the wind
from its hooks like bought meat.

Winter is come with its strict fur shell,
bespoke wind. Cropped outlines

of pleasure craft tend toward
the sandy point and its ethereal edgings.

Once we pass the horizon there is
not a question of turning back, but

placing your hand just so. Where
our audience of one, rapt, bemused,

tardy for another appointment, forgives
our trespasses and trespasses

right back.

The Feed

1.

Here in the thought where traffic lies down,
afternoon snakes northbound, breaks—

no, broken, hissing, by light. The river is
penned and preening, a lash of fulminance

nothing but itself. Sky's peach highlights
tucked in for the underneath. Playing at

holy thief, the viscous minutes swarm streetside
thistle over and trash dirt sparrows

as so much bauble. Skin folds and
snags while night nudges its borderless

knives into day. Ride the surface drag,
says our dress: boats idle-face the water

and wind sifts itself for itself.

2.

Who hungers for rest would drop himself

dead as so many fat fish. Today, haunted
by a cavernous body, I sit like code

in a cold cocoon. Still, the no-birds roll this
city window, road's whisper-funnel distracts from the

dance & drag of someone else's skiff.
Our clear cut face exposes itself like a moon

to the moon. The moon asniff at horizon's curve—
mine own distracted satellite. So we take

to each pleasure vat, take to the oil poured in
to seal the job of air.

3.
We call this home blowzy names
like calling busses, the surrender-you

to the open eye. Think: flash, cut, shadow fish

taken whole then dismembered to molecules
for the fuel breaking-down gives off.

Here is light's causeway, the leather foot
put down, the sharp getting at

your throat. The patois of seeming slaps
liquid like a dull tongue—even as innumerable windows

burn in high praise to number. Cloud hooks bring
the sky low, name it

like the next argument. The river swallows
another live thing. And you, Swallow, swallow, loop and feed.

Notes

In "Reverent Cha Cha" the line "Take this cup from . . ." is adapted from Eshelman's translation of the Vallejo poem, "Spain, take this cup from me."

The title of "The Sun Is the Country Wherever He Is" is from Stevens.

In "Quarry" the line "Sin is not a negation, but a position" is Kierkegaard's.

The title of "The Giver of Gifts Knows Nothing of the Delights of the Merchant" is from Blake, and its first line is modified from Eshelman's translation of Vallejo.

The epigraph for "Work Song" is from Sidney's "Ye Goat-herd Gods."

Recent Titles from Alice James Books

The Chime, Cort Day
Utopic, Claudia Keelan
Pity the Bathtub Its Forced Embrace of the Human Form,
    Matthea Harvey
Isthmus, Alice Jones
The Arrival of the Future, B.H. Fairchild
The Kingdom of the Subjunctive, Suzanne Wise
Camera Lyrica, Amy Newman
How I Got Lost So Close to Home, Amy Dryansky
Zero Gravity, Eric Gamalinda
Fire & Flower, Laura Kasischke
The Groundnote, Janet Kaplan
An Ark of Sorts, Celia Gilbert
The Way Out, Lisa Sewell
The Art of the Lathe, B.H. Fairchild
Generation, Sharon Kraus
Journey Fruit, Kinereth Gensler
We Live in Bodies, Ellen Doré Watson
Middle Kingdom, Adrienne Su
Heavy Grace, Robert Cording
Proofreading the Histories, Nora Mitchell
We Have Gone to the Beach, Cynthia Huntington
The Wanderer King, Theodore Deppe
Girl Hurt, E.J. Miller Laino
The Moon Reflected Fire, Doug Anderson
Vox Angelica, Timothy Liu
Call and Response, Forrest Hamer
Ghost Letters, Richard McCann
Upside Down in the Dark, Carol Potter
Where Divinity Begins, Deborah DeNicola
The Wild Field, Rita Gabis

ALICE JAMES BOOKS has been publishing exclusively poetry since 1973. One of the few presses in the country that is run collectively, the cooperative selects manuscripts for publication through both regional and national annual competitions. New authors become active members of the cooperative, participating in the editorial decisions of the press. The press, which places an emphasis on publishing women poets, was named for Alice James, sister of William and Henry, whose gift for writing was ignored and whose fine journal did not appear in print until after her death.

TYPESET AND DESIGNED BY MIKE BURTON
PRINTING BY THOMSON-SHORE